Essential Insights To Living Your Best Life

~~~

Mahara Wayman
~~~

Self-Published in Canada by Mahara Wayman

First Press Edition, 2022

Edited by Kimberley Rivando-Robb - RetroScripts
www.retroscripts.ca

ISBN 978-1-7782748-0-0

DEDICATION

Dedicated with love and gratitude to my mother,
Alannah Sinclaire and my mother-in-law, Sharon Wayman.
Both have seen me at my best and worst and love me
unconditionally.

CONTENTS

ACKNOWLEDGMENTS

I couldn't pass the opportunity to acknowledge my deep appreciation to my husband Chris and my children, Sophia and Kayla, for their unwavering support of my dreams. They listened, smiled and told me to go for it. Their encouragement tells me I can do anything and I believe them.

FORWARD

~~~

My name is Sonia Ovenden, and I am an award-winning Transformational Life Coach, a TEDx speaker and author. I have also shared the stage with world-renowned thought leaders, including Les Brown, Mary Morrissey, Gay Hendricks, Natalie Ledwell, Lisa Sasevich and Marisa Peer, to name a few.

I have over 25 years of experience in the personal development industry and am the CEO of my business, Discover The Beauty of You Limited. I have read dozens of non-fiction books over the years and am proud to add Essential Insights To Living Your Best Life to my collection. When Mahara shared her idea for this book with me, I was intrigued about where this would take her.

I first met Mahara in the spring of 2021 when she joined one of my 5-day online workshops. Before the program, we chatted over zoom, and her energy was compelling; I knew I had just met someone special. While working together, I was impressed by her willingness to grow and create the life of her dreams.

Essential Insights To Living Your Best Life is a beautiful book many will relate to. It takes you on a gentle trip through Mahara's life as a daughter, mom and entrepreneur as she shares personal stories highlighting a range of human emotions and the challenges accompanying them. It also allows you look at your life and learn, through the lessons that life throws at us, how to live fully.
~~~

Her willingness to be vulnerable with her light and relatable writing style makes for an enjoyable and thought-provoking read. Coupled with additional exercises, it becomes an experience, a chance to connect with yourself in a new way.

While I could identify to every story, I was most moved by those depicting her relationship with her mother. I could relate, and I am sure you will too. This book will prompt you to see things in your life that, up until now, may have been ignored. It offers beautiful wisdom on being happy and present.

Mahara is the perfect person to write this book as I have watched her work diligently to understand her choices and notice what she is experiencing in her own life. She is passionate about sharing her message with the world because she knows how much it's needed.

I am excited for everyone to experience the journey *Essential Insights To Living Your Best Life* offers. You will laugh, cry and question. Most importantly, you will learn something new about your life and the choices available for you to move forward. And who doesn't want insight like that!

Love and hugs,
Sonia

TIPS TO GET THE MOST FROM THIS BOOK

~~~

This book contains eight personal stories highlighting breakthroughs I have experienced during my journey of self-discovery. Although these stories are unique to my life, they hold teachings that will resonate on some level with each reader.

Here are some best practices for getting the most out of this book:

- Get comfortable and start with the story. For me, that means sinking into my reclining sofa with a doctored coffee at the ready.

- Invite any emotions the story brings up to sit with you for a bit; notice what you are feeling.

- Connect those feelings with an experience you have had. Can you relate to my story?

- Dive into the reflection exercises; they will support you as you gently explore your feelings.

- Explore those answers further with the journal prompts. Free writing is a beautiful way to express yourself; no one ever needs to read it.

- Pull it all together on the appreciation action page. Gratitude alone is lovely, but gratitude with action is powerful.
~~~

CHAPTER 1
~
BEST MOM EVER

“Hello, Hello. Are you there, Mom? It's me, Mahara."

Sound familiar? Judy Blume had the original, and better, iteration, I know. Still, those were my words tonight as I tried in vain to have a phone conversation with my aged mother. She couldn't hear me, wasn't sure which daughter was calling and wanted me to talk to her nurse instead.

"Is it on speaker?" she asks her nurse. "Who's calling? Hello? Hello? I can't hear you. Can you put it on speaker and turn it up?"

As frustration got the better of me, I explained to her nurse, Amy, that I would try her again another time. I wondered where the time had gone as I hung up the phone. I take pride in expressing myself well and making solid connections with people. So, how was it that I was in my mid-fifties and unable to communicate with my 95-year-old mother?

Furthermore, I have always had a close and loving relationship with my mother. However, at that moment, my throat was closing around my words, and my thoughts were spiralling downwards. I couldn't have hung up faster if I tried. I didn't want to be that daughter one second longer. The daughter that her mom didn't hear or perhaps even recognize. The daughter who thought, "Just put in your hearing aid, Mom! I know you have a perfectly good one because my brother just checked it for you." Instead, I gave a stranger an update to pass along; "Please tell her we are all fine. It's cold here. We miss her and hope to see her soon."

I live in a different province than the rest of my family, and we are still struggling to find our balance amid a global pandemic. The chances of me seeing my mom anytime soon are slim to none. Not only am I unable to see or hold her, but she's at that age when her next journey will be her last. The thoughts race through my mind; what will I do if she passes before I can hold her and thank her for being the best mom ever?
I am short of breath all of a sudden.

I didn't have these thoughts when preparing for my father to pass away years ago as he struggled with cancer. For some reason, I managed his illness and inevitable death much better than I am handling my mother's slow demise.

What exactly was I feeling at that moment? Good question. Was I annoyed because I still could not connect with her when I finally got through? Perhaps it was regret that my efforts to be a good daughter were for naught? Wow, now that sounds self-serving! Or was I angry that my mom wasn't behaving the way I wanted? I think I just answered my own question.

Despite my efforts to be honest, thoughtful and enlightened, I was anything but at that moment. The sad truth was that I was inexplicably angry at my mom because she wasn't the mom I needed or wanted. I was resentful that time was slipping away from me and frustrated that the pandemic had kept us apart. I realized then that I was, in fact, angry at myself. My beautiful mother had done nothing wrong and was doing her best in a lousy situation.

My mom suffers from short-term memory loss and dementia. Despite wearing a hearing aid, she also can't hear much and was recently moved from a one-bedroom apartment in a seniors facility to one room in a nursing home. As a result, she is incredibly lonely and afraid; such is her reality.

Twenty-four hours later, I had a slightly better phone call with my mom, with Amy once again playing intermediary. She still couldn't hear me, but she was happy to know I was on the phone. Mom haltingly and loudly asked me a question; I answered, and Amy wrote my answer down. Yes, it was the same few questions asked repeatedly; "Are you happy?", "Where are you living now?", "Sweetheart, when will I see you again?"

Still, without a doubt, for the next 2 minutes at least, she knew that her youngest child was happy, living in Alberta, and wasn't sure when she'd be in BC next. I have chosen to be content with that and forgive myself for yesterday's anger. Today is a better day for this enlightened daughter.

Today, with heartfelt gratitude, I acknowledge how fortunate I am to have her in my life. I am thankful she has such a caring woman looking after her. I choose to remember all the times my mom demonstrated that I was her world, and that she was proud of me. Mom, there is something I need to tell you. I am proud of you. You are, and always have been, the best mom ever.

REFLECTION EXERCISE
CLARITY IS KEY

~~~

We often see in others what we see in ourselves. For example, my mother's inability to hear me clearly showed my inadequacies in communicating. That struck a nerve. I also struggled with accepting the reality that my beloved mom had changed, and our roles had, in essence, reversed.

Here are a few questions that may help you understand why a particular event has you in knots. Clarity is everything! You may also come to see a lesson for yourself in the experience. What situation or event, either recent or from your past, still has you upset and/or confused?

- What were you feeling at the moment?
- Were those feelings a surprise?
- Who were those feelings directed at?
- When were those feelings the strongest? From the beginning, or perhaps after some time passed?
- How did the situation and your response relate to what's most important to you?
- What was it about the other person/people's behaviour that triggered your response?
- What could be an opportunity for growth for you?
~~~

JOURNAL PROMPTS

~~~

Recently I have been feeling very…

I'm feeling this way because…

"Never be afraid to speak your truth, for your truth will light the world." *Mahara*

ACTION FOR APPRECIATION

~~~

I am so thankful for Amy's help in communicating with my mom. I am beyond grateful for all the work her nurses do daily to keep her comfortable. I value family and consider mom's nurses as part of our family. My action to highlight my appreciation was to send a small thank you note to the floor nurses in my mother's nursing home.

- What are you thankful for after reading "Best Mom Ever" and working through the follow-up?
- What action can you take to show your appreciation?
- Who will benefit and how?

CHAPTER 2

~

A PROMISE TO MYSELF

I happened upon a picture of myself when I was about 6 or 7 years old and had the most bizarre reaction. I welled up with tears. Considering I was sitting on the couch, watching TV with my husband, this took us both by surprise. It's not as though I haven't seen the picture recently; it pops up now and then in my photos. I remember thinking I looked like a sweet little pumpkin, and my next thought was, "Jesus, what the hell happened to her?"

OK, back up. I thought a myriad of things in that flash. Despite looking solemn in this photo, I was a happy little girl. The youngest of 4 children with (as mentioned before) the best mom ever and the most incredible dad!

I grew up in Jamaica and lived in England for a short time before emigrating to Canada when I was almost 10. I had puppy dogs and kitty cats and was close to my siblings. I remember my brother Graham and I routinely played with our respective Barbie and GI Joe dolls in the front yard. I also remember my older sister, Zoe, sneaking me out of my bedroom window after being grounded for ripping up my playing cards.

We often had family vacations at my aunt's cottage on the island's north coast, where I skylarked with my cousins at every opportunity. I was loved, lacked for nothing and repeatedly told that I could be anything I wanted; what a lucky girl I was.

All through my life, I have had great friends and loving relationships. So why, I ask myself, did I automatically make such a scathing remark about that little girl, all grown up? Was I trying to be funny? To who? Myself?

"Get a life, Mahara!" Oops, there I go again using humour to negate the heaviness of the question.

So what do I consciously say to myself today? Typically I keep it short and sassy like "You rock, girlfriend!" or "Watch me." I am big on the power of language and routinely remind all who listen to their silent script to make sure they are saying nice things and not being such a meanie. After my wake-up call, I realized I needed to take my advice.

I am living proof that no matter how together, enlightened, and grounded you are, you can still slip into the dark zone of self-flagellation. That behaviour is insidious; it creeps into your awareness when least expected and leaves a bitter taste. Which, considering I had an excellent dinner topped off with Haagen Dazs, is heartbreaking! I had not treated myself to the gourmet ice cream for years and tonight's tears risked marring the experience.

As any good coach would, I asked myself why that comment and why now? It's true that I am tired and have been overdosing on self-help books about emotional agility (thank you, Susan David) and being a badass, according to Jen Sincero. That should have made me even more aware. Is it possible that my inner script is coming to the surface because of my reading? If that is the case, I may add credits to my Audible account and ice cream to my freezer.

Honestly, I am delighted with my life and like myself, warts and all. I still have loving relationships and am blessed with a beautiful family. Regardless, I have decided to print out that picture and keep it handy to talk to her nicely, as often as possible, just in case - a promise to my grown-up self.

What would I say?

Baby girl, I'm proud of you.

Mahara, you mattered then, and you matter now.

Wow, you grew into a super cool chick.

Love that frock!

REFLECTION EXERCISE
THE POWER OF LANGUAGE

~~~

Language is powerful and your choice of words, used consciously or not, tells the world a story. This exercise may help you understand if that story is the one you want to keep telling. Remember, it's OK to feel a certain way, but you don't need to label yourself that way.

- What are three positive words you use to describe yourself?

    I am:
    I am this way because:
    I love this about myself because:

- What are three negative words you use to describe yourself?

    I am:
    I chose this word because:

- Rewrite the sentence with "I notice I sometimes feel______" at the start of the sentence:

- Can you feel the difference between your negative "I am" sentence and your negative "I notice" sentence?
~~~

JOURNAL PROMPTS

~~~

Regardless of how I have felt in the past, today I…

My new favourite words to describe me are…

"Language is powerful, choose your words wisely." *Mahara*

ACTION FOR APPRECIATION

~~~

I felt bad and was so surprised by this experience that I was determined to do something nice for myself. To highlight my appreciation for the lesson in self-talk, I purchased a dictionary/thesaurus. I use it regularly to learn better words to describe myself and the world as I see it. I also periodically give pictures of myself a high-five when I see them. Thank you, Mel Robbins, author of The High-Five Habit.

- What are you thankful for after reading "A Promise To Myself" and working through the follow-up?
- What action can you take to show your appreciation?
- Who will benefit and how?

CHAPTER 3

~

COURAGE AND MOTHERHOOD

I always wanted children; in fact, I wanted kids more than marriage. Happily, I got both. However, the naivety of my teenage dreams of being a mom became glaringly apparent within my first year of motherhood. No one talked about lack of sleep or leaking breasts being the norm. No one hinted at how hard it would be to consistently do the right thing, say the right words or even cook a decent meal.

Interestingly, sitting down to write this piece was the first time that I consciously put the words courage and motherhood together. What took me so long?

I am the mother of two incredible young women aged 23 and 18. Here are some things I've learned about courage along the way and how it came knocking on the door of motherhood, looking for a home.

To begin with, I define courage simply as doing the thing that frightens you. Because I had always wanted to be a mom, it never occurred to me to be afraid of motherhood. It wasn't until I had kids that I realized just how much courage it took each day to be the mom I wanted to be: present, loving, understanding, and forgiving. Let me reiterate; it takes courage to be a good mom, and courage comes in many forms.

Can we all agree that it's a massive leap of faith to promise your tiny, squalling child an extraordinary life? It may not be that easy to deliver on that promise when reality sets in. When my girls were little, I got away with a lot because they didn't question me; their inability to talk worked in my favour.

The challenges started when they began to communicate and learned the dreaded words "why" and "no." Some conversations deteriorated even further when they began to question, extrapolate, reason, and consequently point out my lack thereof. "That's not what you said yesterday!"

How do you explain to your child that sometimes, as a mom, I don't need a good reason to change my mind? These tearful exchanges invariably left me more unsettled than the girls. I was the one questioning my parenting skills and would inevitably wonder what my mom would have done in my place. My mother, by the way, is the best mom ever.

One day, when my oldest was in grade school, I found her on the verge of tears on my bed. When I asked what was wrong, she haltingly announced that she needed to start exercising because a kid at school taunted her with "you're fat!" At first, amidst anger and shock, I didn't immediately understand my part in this drama. It took me a couple of days to realize the disservice I had inadvertently done to my daughter.

You see, I had always been self-deprecating about my weight in front of her. She heard me flippantly say things like "God, I'm fat" and "I need to lose weight." When she looked up at me from my bed with tears on her face and asked, "Mummy, am I fat?" I died a little inside. I gathered her in my arms and, while gently rocking her, quietly told her that she wasn't overweight and didn't need to diet. She was ten years old and hurting. I was forty-three years old and crushed.

After railing at the injustice of schoolyard bullies, I was forced to admit to the hard truth that I was the catalyst for this sad situation. It was tough for me to accept my part in my daughter's skewered body image. I had inadvertently taught her the mistaken importance of looking a certain way or being a certain weight. Shame on me!

What if I had taught her to love herself regardless of her weight? That her self-worth should be connected to her spirit instead of her shape? Would she have laughed in that child's face and moved on? Perhaps she wouldn't have even viewed the comment as hurtful. What other failings would come to light if I admitted to that failure? I thought I was a great mom; hell, I still believe that, but boy, I know now that wasn't always the case, at least in that respect.

Admitting that I needed to change how I spoke to myself was difficult and scary. I was afraid to try. It took courage to look at my failings, real or perceived, as I developed into the mom I am today.

It also took courage to go against what other moms said or did. I had to choose to stick to my guns and not bend when the tears came, or the pleading started.
It has taken years, but I have changed my narrative around my health and weight and am very conscious of the words I use today.

What have I learned from this introspection? First, I've learned that it's OK to struggle with being a mom. I realize it is a blessing to have created opportunities to face your fears and insecurities. How wonderful to be courageous even if no one knows. I have also learned that being a mom is the most significant role I will ever have.

Today, when my girls smile and tell me they love me, I smile back and say a silent thank you. I also acknowledge that all I can ask of myself at any given moment is my best, and often, my best takes courage.

REFLECTION EXERCISE
WHAT COURAGE MEANS TO YOU

~~~

Courage comes in many forms and means different things to different people. It is the stuff of legends and the subplot of our most beloved stories and movies. It's also the subplot of your story. Catalogue a lifetime of your acts of courage and acknowledge your superpower.

- How do you define courage?
- Who or what taught you this definition?
- How has your courage shown up in your life?

Include:

- Your age
- What you did
- Why it was courageous
- The result your act of courage had on the rest of your life
~~~

JOURNAL PROMPTS

~~~

I am so proud of myself because…

I'm feeling this way because…

"Courage is a form of personal currency that pays dividends in the face of adversity." *Mahara*

ACTION FOR APPRECIATION

~~~

I am beyond thankful that I have a role model in my mother. I modelled her unconditional love and level of consciousness with my children as best I could. I often thought, "What would mom do?" Years later, to highlight my appreciation for this, I called her and thanked her. I also thanked my children and apologized for the times I may have gotten it wrong.

- What are you thankful for after reading "Courage and Motherhood" and working through the follow-up?
- What action can you take to show your appreciation?
- Who will benefit and how?

CHAPTER 4
~
MY CHILDREN ARE MORE INTELLIGENT THAN ME

As life often does, it brought to my attention a lesson that hadn't occurred to me; my children are more intelligent than me. As a mother, I suspect I'm not alone in this epiphany, but that doesn't make it any less uncomfortable.

I have two girls who are five years apart in age. As children, mealtimes were often a trial; one would sit head bowed slowly, picking at everything on her plate, while the other enthusiastically ate everything except the vegetables. She happily declared that she no eat "begetables." "Oh yes, you do!" was my go-to, lofty reply. There ensued a battle of wills that I usually lost, with my explanation that children needed their vegetables to grow big and tall habitually falling on deaf ears.

I recall the time Kayla reminded me that she didn't like cauliflower, and my automatic response was to exclaim, "What's not to like, for goodness sake?". It hardly has any taste and is an excellent base for everyone's favourite, grated cheese. This produced an ultimate staredown match with my youngest. Eyes locked with mine, she gently picked up a tiny cauliflower floret and placed it in her mouth. Without moving anything but her mouth, she began to chew, once with slow deliberation, then once more with lips screwed tight. Her next movement was to swallow the tiny piece of mush. Success! I thought with pride. Alas, it was not meant to be. Kayla proceeded to throw up on the table and herself. When she had finished, she glared at me through lowered lids and quietly said, "I don't eat begetables, Mama." "Oh, for God's sake, Kayla!" I erupted, the pride draining from me. This incident was nothing out of the ordinary because, as a mom of young kids, I was constantly cleaning up after them and cursing under my breath.

My discovery of her acumen came months later at the local swimming pool. While getting dried off after frolicking with pool toys, she walked to the automatic hand dryer on the wall. She slowly reached out with one of her hands and stretched up onto her tippy toes. With a squeal of success, she smacked the large button, turning on the stream of warm air. With genuine delight, I said out loud something along the lines of, "Oh, you big grown-up girl!" She promptly turned to face me and replied, "Yes, I am and with no begetables either!" There was a moment of amused silence in the changing room.

The other mothers looked at me with sympathy and genuine merriment. They knew exactly what I was thinking. With smiles that ranged from slight to beaming, they understood my dilemma and commiserated with my plight. At that moment, we were connected as only young mothers can be. Without a doubt, we knew that my child was more intelligent than me.

Ironic reveal:

Today my daughter, who refused to eat "begetables", is following a vegan lifestyle and only eats vegetables!

REFLECTION EXERCISE
LAUGHTER IS THE BEST MEDICINE

~~~

When you're in the throws of motherhood sometimes there isn't any room for humour. That would require slowing down and a totally different mindset. I may have smirked along with the other moms, but I was more tired and frustrated than amused. However, years later, I see the humour and am grateful for that. Laughing is a beautiful way to connect with the kid in you. Did you know that on an average day, kids laugh more than ten times as much as adults? Here are some questions to bring awareness to the laughter in your life.

- What are your favourite TV sitcoms?
- Was there a lot of laughter in your home growing up?
- When was the last time you belly laughed?

JOURNAL PROMPTS

~~~

The funniest thing I ever did ...

The funniest thing I ever saw…

"There is a space between moments where the magic happens. Look for the magic and laugh." *Mahara*

ACTION FOR APPRECIATION

~~~

Today I recognize how much I need laughter in my life and have chosen to look for it at every opportunity. I don't take myself too seriously and am usually the first to crack a smile instead of a frown when things become stressful. My action for appreciation was to happily sit down with my husband to watch his favourite show, "Coronation Street," an English soap opera that I find hilarious. What began as a lark has turned into years of shared smiles and some raucous laughter, helped along, I'm sure, by channel surfing and watching "Whose Line Is It Anyway?" during the commercial breaks.

- What are you thankful for after reading "My Children Are More Intelligent Than me" and working through the follow-up?
- What action can you take to show your appreciation?
- Who will benefit and how?
~~~

CHAPTER 5
~
MEET MY INNER SABOTEUR AND DIVA

I remember when I met my Inner Saboteur and Inner Diva, two prominent voices in my head. I was chatting with some new friends at a retreat and had an epiphany that, true to form, rocked my world. Perhaps it'll rock yours too.

Before I get into that, let me remind you of my background. I am a happy, successful entrepreneur known for wearing a few hats. I'm an author, motivational speaker and life coach who supports and teaches women to harness their voice, declare their worth and thrive in their lives.

I'm passionate about the importance of listening to your inner dialogue, owning your truth without judgement and rewriting your story if the feelings and emotions it evokes no longer serve you. Knowing this, can you imagine my surprise when I realized that I desperately needed my coaching? Now, that was a mic-drop moment.

As I participated in the retreat and absorbed the lessons, activities, and soul-stirring conversations, I identified - maybe for the first time - my Inner Saboteur and Inner Diva. Their low gravel tones sent shivers down my spine as I heard them say things like "You aren't good enough" and "Listen to you talk. It's no wonder they don't respect you."

Let me be clear; I am very mindful of how I speak to myself, but I never understood who was behind the voices in my head or that they were operating behind a beautiful mask of helpfulness. They wanted to protect me from further pain and often gave off "I got your back, girlfriend!" vibes. However, I now understand their thoughts and comments were holding me back from moving through long-ago hurts. I also acknowledge that I am the one that fashioned the mask and gave it power. Oh, the indignity of that realization! As I listened, I realized their voices began long ago, with a furtive whisper in the dark and a lonely classroom.

How could I have created and then listened to these scathing attacks, and more importantly, now that I recognized them for what they were, how could I allow it to continue? I couldn't, and this was the birth of my epiphany.

Stepping into this new realization, I see these constant companions for what they are. Essentially, they are the young and wounded parts of me attempting to protect me from further hurt or shame. They try to influence my behaviour whenever they feel I am threatened. Inner Saboteur and Inner Diva are simply the voices of my fears, twisted observations and incorrect assumptions created through the lens of a child. They have been with me for a long time, and I often listen to their advice. I question my worth. I shut up, look away and don't always lean into anything uncomfortable or unknown.

Inner Saboteur worked hard over the years to guard me. She insidiously shared her opinion on my abilities and supposed transgressions. Her best friend, Inner Diva, loved finishing my sentences and creating whole narratives to support her instead of me. Talk about adding insult to injury! However, Inner Diva knew I would let her talk because sometimes I was too scared to speak for myself. Her way with words convinced me every time. She exaggerated, and I bought the story without question. I have chosen to thank them, as I know they were only trying to protect and keep me safe.

I can't help but wonder, though, what opportunities I may have missed along the way. They had a starring role in my past, but I only see a supporting role for them moving forward. They no longer have ringside seats in my life. Instead, various nurturing people have taken those front row center spots at my proverbial table; only my faithful supporters have that privilege.

My Inner Saboteur and Inner Diva can now look forward to a life with long bouts of silence. While they probably will be chit-chatting to each other in the background, I won't hear them as loudly as I once did. When their voices begin to pick up steam, I will listen but gently explain why I no longer need them, and I'll stand true to who I am, even if I get hurt or make a mistake. It's not a mistake if you learn from it; I am all about learning and growing these days. I'm sure they will be wondering why I don't listen to them as much anymore, and that's OK. I don't need to explain myself. With a twinkle in my eye, I acknowledge the power I gave to these inner voices, but things are different now. I have regained that authority and, instead, am the motivation behind my actions.

Do you know what's interesting, though?

Despite their claims to the contrary, neither of them is very smart. I say that because it only took one well-crafted afternoon of conversation to dismantle years of deception; theirs, not mine. All I needed were the proper conversations with the right women at the perfect time to understand what I had created and why.

I know they will never leave me altogether, but I have told them they must be prepared to work with me instead of against me. Whenever I'm interrupted or an attempt to silence me arises, it's them, not me, that risks being summarily dismissed. My goal is to listen with tenderness and remind them I am in charge.

You see, part of the magic of that fateful afternoon of conversation was a recognition of my sacred voice, which will roar on my invitation. It will drown out any protestations or vulgar platitudes that spew from their mouths. My divine voice squashes their squeaks, throwaways, and lies and blankets theirs with loving forgiveness.

So I invite them to stand silently beside me as I move into my purpose. I think of them as my shadow selves and they will be closed-mouthed and opened-hearted observers of my greatness. I want them to nod, look at each other with pride as I tiptoe gently, and then march with knees high into a life full of fearless passion and unfiltered creativity. When I am bursting with excitement, they will be silently bursting with excitement too. When I am crying in frustration, they will silently cry alongside me. As I embrace the unknown with trepidation, they, too, will silently embrace the unknown.

A momentous thing happened that day; my world was rocked and I couldn't be happier.

REFLECTION EXERCISE
MEET AND GREET

~~~

Stop, breathe and listen is the order of the day when you think you may be listening to your Inner Diva or Saboteur. Note, according to my friend and fellow coach, Jodie Graham, CEC (who designed the retreat and created the content referenced in my story), Inner Diva and Saboteur are the most common speakers in your head and the ones this exercise will reference.

Should vs Could - Thank you, Louise Hay, author of "You Can Heal Your Life." One way your Inner Saboteur talks to you is to use the word "should."

- List the times you told yourself you SHOULD have done/ thought/ felt something.

E.g., I should have gotten that raise.

- List the same again using COULD instead of SHOULD.

E.g., I could have gotten that raise.

- Did you notice a difference in how both statements felt?

Uncover The Facts - Thank you, Brenee Brown, author of "Rising Strong." Our Inner Diva likes to fill in the blanks and often exaggerates a story.

- Describe in detail a story you have told yourself that has left you feeling angry, disappointed or worried.
~~~

- Next, bold or underline everything you know that is 100% true. Do not bold or underline anything that is an opinion or a guess.
- Now look to see how much of that narrative is not bold or underlined, and by default, you do not know if true.
- Notice your feelings when you see the revised and stripped-down factual version of your story.

Here's an example.

> Last week I was left off the agenda for our weekly meeting at work, and because of that, I couldn't present my new idea to the department. My boss doesn't like me and isn't interested in hearing my thoughts. She doesn't respect me, my creativity or what I bring to the team. She ignored my attempts to catch her eye during the meeting and purposely ignored my follow-up email that afternoon.
>
> **Last week I was left off the agenda for our weekly meeting at work, and because of that, I couldn't present my new idea to the department.** My boss doesn't like me and isn't interested in hearing my thoughts. She doesn't respect me, my creativity or what I bring to the team. She ignored my attempts to catch her eye during the meeting and purposely ignored my follow-up email that afternoon.

I was genuinely shocked when I realized much of my anger was based on assumptions. I couldn't argue with the facts, but I could rethink my reaction, seeing as though I was reacting to a made-up story I was telling myself.

JOURNAL PROMPTS

~~~

Tell a story about your Inner Saboteur or Inner Diva, and consider the following points:

- What do they look like?
- What are they wearing?
- What is their favourite saying?

"Harness your voice, declare your worth and flourish in all you do." *Mahara*

ACTION FOR APPRECIATION

~~~

This experience led to copious amounts of self-care. I took long and relaxing bubble baths while I tried to sort out the most pressing examples of times I had allowed these parts of me to flourish. I chose to be gentle and loving in little ways. I think there was even a time or two of decadent chocolate!

- What are you thankful for after reading "Meet My Inner Saboteur And Diva" and working through the follow-up?
- What action can you take to show your appreciation?
- Who will benefit and how?

CHAPTER 6

~

NAUGHTY GIRLS DON'T GET DINNER

During the middle of the pandemic, life took me to a woman's retreat in Central Alberta. The weather couldn't have been better for the end of September, with clear blue skies, crisp autumn air and mild temperatures greeting me on my arrival. The long gravel driveway crinkled in anticipation of new guests, and the still lush, sprawling green grounds of the 4- H Club welcomed us to call it home for the next three days. The gentle slope of the lawn wickedly beckoned this 55-year-old to contemplate falling to her knees and unceremoniously rolling herself to the bottom like she used when she was a little girl.

With tote bags and bedding in hand, I marvelled at the beauty around me. A deep forest of statuesque trees wearing their best yellow and gold finery dwarfed the main building where we would meet met each morning at 6:30 am. While we meditated and did Nia - a beautiful new-to-me movement practice - in the chilly basement, the real work happened upstairs in a bright, large, outdated room.

Floor-to-ceiling windows trimmed in oak lead out to an unadorned wood porch, begging for a fresh coat of paint. The other three walls, plain and panelled, were peppered with a photo history of the Club and white poster sheets, scotched taped somewhat haphazardly containing instructions for the various retreat activities.

Day three of the retreat found me sitting at my round banquet table, artfully covered with brown paper to hide the knicks and age spots befitting a table from the 1970s. Evidence of my activities lay strewn in front of me: assorted highlighters, brightly coloured post-it notes, pieces of cut-out magazines - the beginnings of a vision board, and a water bottle with lipstick stains.

With only eight of us sharing the open space, I figured everyone knew my name by now, so I had no concern about repositioning my personalized nameplate. Decorated with stickers and fancy pens, it stood awkwardly facing the back wall as we shared our ah-ha moments and deep personal insights.

In a fascinating and straightforward exercise, we recalled an event from our past we felt was the catalyst for a limiting belief in our present.

The instructions posted directly to my left were as follows:

- What is a limiting belief affecting you today?

"Only one?" I thought as I repositioned my chair to face left.

- Can you think of an event from your past that may explain this belief?

Oh, this is interesting. I slumped a bit, wrapping my black shawl tightly around my shoulders.

- How has that belief affected your life?

Thinking, Ok, I need a drink! I turned to face forward once again and had my epiphany for the day.

In what felt like only a few seconds, I went from a grounded and grinning life coach to a heartbroken little girl, hungry after missing supper.

When the facilitator noticed my pale face and brimming eyes, she gently asked me to share. I took a few deep breaths and wiped my eyes before recalling the only time my beautiful mother ever laid a hand on me. I had stuck my tongue out at her in a fit of pique, and she pulled me up by one arm and gave me a spanking on my backside. I'm not sure who was more surprised or upset as we glared at each other with solitary tears of indignation rolling down my face.

For my rudeness, I was banished to my bedroom without supper.
With seven pairs of eyes glued to mine, I concluded in halting sentences that naughty girls went hungry and acknowledged that little me had drawn a misguided correlation between behaviour and hunger. While planted long ago, that belief is still buried deep within me today.

I still loathe feeling hungry, and now I think I understand why.

REFLECTION EXERCISE
IDENTIFYING YOUR BLOCKS

~~~

Identifying my blocks was incredibly humbling and powerful. I encourage you to be open to the exercise below and trust that your inner wisdom will give you the answers you seek.

- What is a limiting belief affecting you today?
- Can you think of an event from your past that may explain this belief?
- How has that belief affected your life?

Here is my example from the retreat.

- I can't easily lose weight.
- I was punished once as a little girl for being naughty and went without supper and was hungry.
- I am an emotional eater and hate being hungry. I rarely let myself feel hunger and have struggled to maintain a healthy weight most of my adult life.
~~~

JOURNAL PROMPTS

~~~

I forgive myself for the misunderstanding…

The truth is that...

"Don't let dark thoughts from yesterday colour today's masterpiece." *Mahara*

ACTION FOR APPRECIATION

~~~

This revelation was undeniably an uncomfortable experience, but I was very thankful for it. I knew right away that it was a game-changer for me in so many ways. As a way to honour that, I chose to write about it. I decided to journal, at length, my feelings and other ideas that sprang from the experience. It may not seem like a huge appreciation action, but it was a gift to me and one way to honour that little girl.

- What are you thankful for after reading "Naughty Girls Don't Get Dinner" and then working through the follow-up?
- What action can you take to show your appreciation?
- Who will benefit and how?

CHAPTER 7
~
IN AND OUT OF THE FADE

Can one ever be fully prepared to witness your mother's mind jump to and fro, fading in and out of that place of no return? My mother was a woman of strength, the matriarch of the family, and the go-to person for advice, love, hugs and acceptance. She was articulate and intelligent, ever the reader that sparked my love of reading. I remember spending hours talking about books that we had recently enjoyed (or not). She regularly contributed poetry to her retirement home's monthly newsletter and admits that writing kept her sharp. A nature lover, she would invite the reader to listen to the birds as they spoke or to find comfort in the seasons changing, as leaves fell from trees. To this day, I still ask her what she's reading, and it continues to be a significant tie and source of joy for us.

Short-term memory loss wasn't a surprise; I saw it coming and accepted my mom's condition as a matter of course for one of her age. She was 96 years old last month, and yesterday, I was challenged to be what she needed in her moment of disconnection and fear. Did I have what it would take to navigate this conversation and not exacerbate the problem, leaving me frustrated and angry? I flashed back to previous conversations where I innocently corrected her, thinking that was what she needed - then having to back-peddle when I realized my mistake.

When the phone rang, and I saw it was her, I was genuinely excited. I wanted to tell her about my latest article and ask for her feedback, a.k.a love and acceptance. I answered the phone with a heartfelt "Hi, Mummy!" but after her first few sentences, my delight changed to a sinking, "Oh no!". I knew she wasn't in a good place, and my wants would have to take a back seat. It was time for me to pull up my big girl panties and be the daughter that my mom needed.

Our phone call began with a tentative, "Mahara, are you there?" and moved quickly into her whispering, "I have something to tell you, and it may be hard for you to hear." My heart plummeted into my stomach, and I felt the slow burn of anxiety begin to weave its way back up to my throat.

She caught my attention because I couldn't imagine anything she had to say as "hard to hear." I was wrong.

My mother told me that when she woke up that morning, she didn't know where she was or why she was there. She panicked and, after looking around her room, saw my name and number on a board, remembered I was her baby and called me straight away. I was heartbroken for her, recognizing how scary that must have been not to remember her surroundings and having to frantically grasp for a familiarity. Thankfully, my name and number were a lifeline for her at that moment.

I am a life coach currently studying to be certified in Coaching Mastery, and one of my recent modules was around acceptance and forgiveness. Thank God because, after my initial panic at how to best support her in this conversation, I accepted the situation and gave her what I knew she needed; complete approval.

I thanked her for calling me and assured her I was prepared for whatever she wanted to share. After her initial confession (for that is how it sounded to me - as if it was her fault she couldn't remember), I acknowledged how gut-wrenching that must have been for her and how happy I was that she had called. As I listened to her whispered, trembling voice, I also told her I was proud of her, understanding the strength it took to pick up the phone and admit her truth. After a few minutes, her voice became more assertive. With gentle prodding, she was able to tell me things that she remembered: we were Jamaicans living in Canada, I was her youngest, and she loves to drive.

That was the start of her journey out of her fade and into her present. Side note; that lasted about 10 minutes. Hooray! 10 minutes of normalcy as we captured the feeling of our relationship, despite the story she told. Some of her memories were fictitious, but I chose to jump into her story with both feet instead of expecting her to enter mine. It's enough for me, and judging by the lilt soon evidenced in her voice, it was enough for her too.

I found it interesting that the minute I accepted the situation without judgement (unlike previous phone calls with her), I felt lighter in spirit and fully present. She came to life in that instant, and her voice's tenor reflected that. Instead of sounding confused and sad, she sounded connected and upbeat. She even cracked a joke about her memory. Was she completely coherent? Absolutely not. Was she happy at that moment? I think so. Will she experience this journey in and out of her fade again? I am sure of it. When that time comes, hopefully, she will see my name and number and remember once more who I am as she starts to dial.

I look forward to that call, as I now understand it is a gift to choose to be present without judgment, a gift for her and me. I won't correct her if she wants to think she still drives her Volkswagen. It makes me smile to hear her speak like that because when she does, she's Mummy.

I don't need to remind my mother of what she has lost; that would be cruel. I do not need to confuse her with what hasn't happened. That would be silly. All I need is to meet her where she is, in the present, with all the love I have for her, the best mom ever.

REFLECTION EXERCISE
COMPASSIONATE SELF-FORGIVENESS

~~~

"In And Out Of The Fade" was a last-minute addition to the book. I was beginning to explore the idea of complete acceptance with forgiveness, and, as the universe often does, it gave me that phone call as an opportunity for serious growth. I saw and felt how easy it was to be fully present without anger or resentment. I accepted it as the ultimate gift.

Here is an exercise to help navigate your relationship with acceptance and judgment. It is based on Alyssa Nobriga's Coaching Certification and includes a forgiveness statement from the University of Santa Monica.

- Identify a situation or event that upsets you whenever you think about it?

E.g., *My mom is old and lonely.*

- Break it down to the basics of what happened and how you felt.

E.g., *My mom just called really upset because she is losing her memory, and I feel lost and frustrated trying to help her.*

- Take your feelings and identify the judgements around them.

E.g., *I'm feeling anger, frustration, shame, and regret.*
~~~

My judgements are:

I should know how to help Mom at that moment.
I should be more understanding.
I should be happy to talk to her regardless of her situation.
I should make more time for her; after everything she done for me.
I am not good daughter anymore.

- Imagine you are a small child in this situation and have just vented your feelings from the last answer. As an adult that loves the younger you, what would you say to comfort them?

E.g., *Sweetheart, you are doing your best.*
You are a wonderful daughter.
You are learning as you go.
Mummy loves you no matter what.

- Take a deep breath and connect with the love and compassion in your heart. Embrace compassionate self-forgiveness for any judgments or limiting conclusions your mind made up about you, someone else or a situation by saying:

  "I forgive myself for buying into the misunderstanding that" (insert your judgement here)

  E.g., *I am not a good daughter.*

  Continue with, "The truth is" (insert current truth here)

  E.g., *I am doing my best in a difficult situation, and mom knows I love her.)*

JOURNAL PROMPTS

~~~

Reoccurring judgements I have about myself are …

The truth is that...

"When you let go of judgment, you instantly create acceptance and are fully present." *Mahara*

ACTION FOR APPRECIATION

~~~

Because of this experience, I chose to add a particular component to my mindfulness practice. At night, after a short meditation, I ask myself, "What judgement came up for me today and why?" Doing this reminds me that judgements are normal, and I am worth the effort it will take to recognize them and understand how I can move away from them.

- What are you thankful for after reading "In And Out Of The Fade" and then working through the follow-up?
- What action can you take to show your appreciation?
- Who will benefit and how?

CHAPTER 8

~

SEE YOU ON THE FLIP SIDE

Throwaway comments are sometimes the switch that turns your life upside down yet right-side out.

During the global pandemic in late 2021, I was word-doodling (daydreaming with a pen) and suddenly glimpsed my future self living my dream.

I said out loud with a wicked grin, "See you on the flip side." It was only later that I realized the power within that throwaway comment. At that moment, I decided I would change and become the vision of myself found in my word doodle regardless of what was happening around the globe.

It's August 2024, and the pock-marked pandemic is behind us. I am living my divine purpose as an author, motivational speaker, and empowerment coach, basking on the sands of my secluded beach in Jamaica. More on that later.

The world didn't go back to normal after the COVID pandemic, and neither did I, which was a good thing. While cloistered in my house for those long, uncertain two years, I made the courageous choice to surrender. With guidance and a boatload of trust, I embarked on a journey to rival that of the Goddess Psyche and read everything I could get my hands on. I connected with brave women worldwide and explored what it meant to be me. I wrote and voiced that throwaway comment, and while not nearly as enlightened as that Greek Goddess, I have moved closer to my inner butterfly and today feel entirely at home in my altered reality.

The reality of the world has also changed. After the pandemic upheaval, people I meet today have come full circle and are again smiling and excited to connect face to face. The buzz is on the street again, not only on the digital highway; surprisingly, the prose is light and filled with promise. Anger and mistrust take a second string, with acceptance and gratitude leading the charge.

Communities shop locally, professionals work less and play more, while children learn organically. Our weakest are held, nursed and given homes and our strongest share their wisdom and fortunes. One oldtimer cackled to himself recently, "Dis is how we a gowan when me a pickney!" That's Jamaican for "This is how we did it my day!" I watched as his friends in the nursing home nodded their heads in agreement.

Most people know that I am Jamaican; those who know me well have heard of my longing to return home, and my closest understand my need to establish myself and my family there at some point in my life. It took the shake-up of the pandemic to make that a reality.

The windows are open in my bright yellow oceanfront villa in Jamaica, and I smell the ocean's soft, salty breeze as it caresses my face. I see the blindingly blue sky peppered with fluffy white clouds. The sea of turquoise blue is topped with frolicking white-capped waves that gently kiss the shores of my secluded beach as they roll in for a respite. I hear the faint sizzle of the water as it recedes. My gaze rests upon the well-worn path that leads from the house to the white sand beach dotted with almond trees. On the other side of the trail sits our tennis court and an infinity pool that I enjoy daily.

The front of the house sports an assortment of my favourite fruit trees: Guinep, Mango, Tamarind, Otaheite Apple, Guava, and Ackee, to name a few! My garden is overflowing with colours: yellow orchids, red hibiscus, pink bougainvillea and our national flower, Lignum Vitae, my purple princess. A flagpole stands tall and sports the Canadian flag, the Jamaican flag and a flag showing my business logo as an homage to my work and acknowledging how that work has contributed to creating this reality. The wind blows, and the flags dance in harmony, a silent tribute to the journey that brought my family and me to this beautiful oasis.

In the distance, I hear my girls happily chatting, my dogs snoring quietly at my feet, sprawled on the polished mahogany floors as the light strains of Bob Marley's "Three Little Birds" tinkle in the background. Someone is playing it on the grand piano.

The walls of our four-bedroom villa are a muted cream with white crown moulding accents. They are the perfect backdrop to the collection of my colourful artwork and those of my favourite local artists, J.Macdonald Henry and Herbie Rose.

My workspace in our upstairs bedroom suite has a gorgeous white custom-made built-in bookshelf. It houses an assortment of loved artwork and favourite books, including some of my own, like my highly acclaimed debut, "Essential Insights To Living Your Best Life" and my recently released children's book "The Adventures of Miranda & Mickey."

A platter of freshly cut mango and papaya sits on my desk alongside a steaming cup of Blue Mountain coffee, my favourite combination of smells to start my day!

My new MacBook is open as I have just booked another client for my current group coaching program. I'm proud to have helped hundreds of people from the UK, Canada, and the United States lead happier, empowered lives.

I love to support children and women's charities with financial donations and silent auction items. In addition, I allow companies to bid for me to be their keynote speaker, and individuals can bid on a three-month 1:1 coaching package with me.

I fulfilled my promise that day and created the reality that was my flip side. When I recall the woman I was, I thank her for showing up then and now, right-side out.

REFLECTION EXERCISE
DEFINE YOUR DREAM

~~~

Unlike the other stories, this is a work of fiction, as it hasn't happened yet. However, I chose to include it because learning to dream was a massive part of my journey. Admitting that I had a dream was more challenging than I expected, but it was a beautiful exercise and continues to feel like the icing on the lovely cupcake that is my empowered life.

Here are some questions to help you get clear on your dream so it can move to the front and center of your world instead of quietly waiting to be noticed in the background.

- If there was NOTHING to stop you, what would you be doing?
- Is this for play or work?
- Where would you live?
- What does your home look like?
- How do you feel looking at that home?
- Who is standing beside you as you gaze at your dream home?
- Describe in detail your kitchen, bedroom, office, etc.
- Do you have neighbours, pets or plants?
- What do you eat for breakfast, lunch or dinner?
- Describe how it feels to honour your dreams by exploring them?
~~~

JOURNAL PROMPTS

~~~

The flip side of my life is...

In my perfect world I...

"Choose to dream and then listen to that little voice that tells you to be brave, be patient and never give up." *Mahara*

ACTION FOR APPRECIATION

~~~

I took a course on building my dreams, and I will forever be grateful to my coach, Sonia Ovenden, who created a safe and fun environment for me to explore and articulate them. I learned that dreams matter and the energy that goes into sustaining them is the energy that brings them to fruition. My action of appreciation was to issue a standing invitation to her to join me in Jamaica!

- What are you thankful for after reading "See You On The Flip Side" and then working through the follow-up?
- What action can you take to show your appreciation?
- Who will benefit and how?

AUTHOR'S NOTE

~~~

It's interesting how much I have learned about myself now that I have chosen to understand the real Me. I waver between wishing I had begun my self-discovery journey sooner and knowing that everything happens at the right time. I consider the things I have learned essential insights to living my best life:

- Clarity is the beginning of every incredible journey. It may not be readily apparent, but it is always worth your effort to have it.
- Self-talk is powerful and recognizing it is priceless. If I am unhappy about something, I now know to check in with my self-talk to gain better insight, aka clarity.
- We are much more courageous than we give ourselves credit for. This journey has shown me that courage comes in many forms, and recognizing when we have chosen courage is a beautiful way to honour ourselves. It can also help change our narrative.
- Laughter is the best medicine, and life is too short to ignore that fact; laugh hard at every opportunity, starting with yourself. Not only will your genuine laughter raise your energy, but it sends a lovely message to the universe.
- One of my most significant discoveries was the latitude I have bestowed upon my shadow selves. Today, I recognize my Inner Saboteur and Inner Diva as essential parts of me
~~~

that warrant grace and forgiveness instead of anger and ridicule.

- Growth can come at any moment and hit like a freight train. However, understanding where my deepest limiting beliefs sprang from was the first step to changing them. I am learning to forgive myself for misunderstandings that my younger self created.

- I allowed real and perceived judgements to keep me from thoroughly enjoying my world. I know that's normal, but I can choose to be fully present without judgement. It takes effort, but it is a sure sign of my growth.
- We are born dreamers, and the possibilities are endless once we permit ourselves to dream big.

I hope my stories have prompted you to ask great questions about yourself and the life you have created. I also hope you are motivated to get to know yourself better so you can navigate any challenge easily and, simultaneously, live your best life.

Here's to you!

Mahara

For more information on Mindfulness With Mahara, please visit my website:
www.minddfulnesswithmahara.com, or follow me on:
www.instagram.com/mindfulnesswithmahara/
www.linkedin.com/in/maharawayman/

Made in the USA
Middletown, DE
08 August 2022

70795561R00031